D1118883

A FIREFLY BOOK

Published by Firefly Books Ltd. 2016

Original French edition opyright © 2014 Larousse
This translated edition © 2016 Firefly Books

All rights reserved. No part of this publication may be reproduced, stored in a retrieval system, or transmitted in any form or by any means, electronic, mechanical, photocopying, recording or otherwise, without the prior written permission of the Publisher.

First printing

Publisher Cataloging-in-Publication Data (U.S.)

A CIP record for this title is available from the Library of Congress

Library and Archives Canada Cataloguing in Publication

A CIP record for this title is available from Library and Archives Canada

Published in the United States by
Firefly Books (U.S.) Inc.
P.O. Box 1338, Ellicott Station
Buffalo, New York 14205

Published in Canada by
Firefly Books Ltd.
50 Staples Avenue, Unit 1
Richmond Hill, Ontario L4B 0A7

Printed in Spain

For Larousse:
Publishing Directors: Isabelle Jeunge-Maynart and Ghislaine Stora; **Editorial Director:** Agnes Busiere; **Edition:** Alice Dauphin; **Cover:** Claire Morel-Fatio; **Photo editing:** Claire Fonder, Camille de Montmorillon, Kelly Lioubchansky, Susan Poy, Aurélie Palumbo; **Layout:** IDT; **Production:** Genevieve Wittmann

SPOT the DIFFERENCE

Find the detail that's different in each scene!

WE HAVE ADDED OR MODIFIED A DETAIL IN EACH OF THE IMAGES IN THIS BOOK.

IF YOU NEED THEM, CLUES AT THE TOP AND THE BOTTOM OF THE PAGE CAN HELP YOU. WHEN THERE ARE TWO CLUES, THE SECOND ONE CAN BE READ WITH A MIRROR.

IF YOU STILL CAN'T FIND IT, ALL THE ANSWERS CAN BE FOUND AT THE END OF THE BOOK.

HAPPY HUNTING!

FIREFLY BOOKS

Don't lose your head.

  Whatever your heart desires...

Time is ticking.

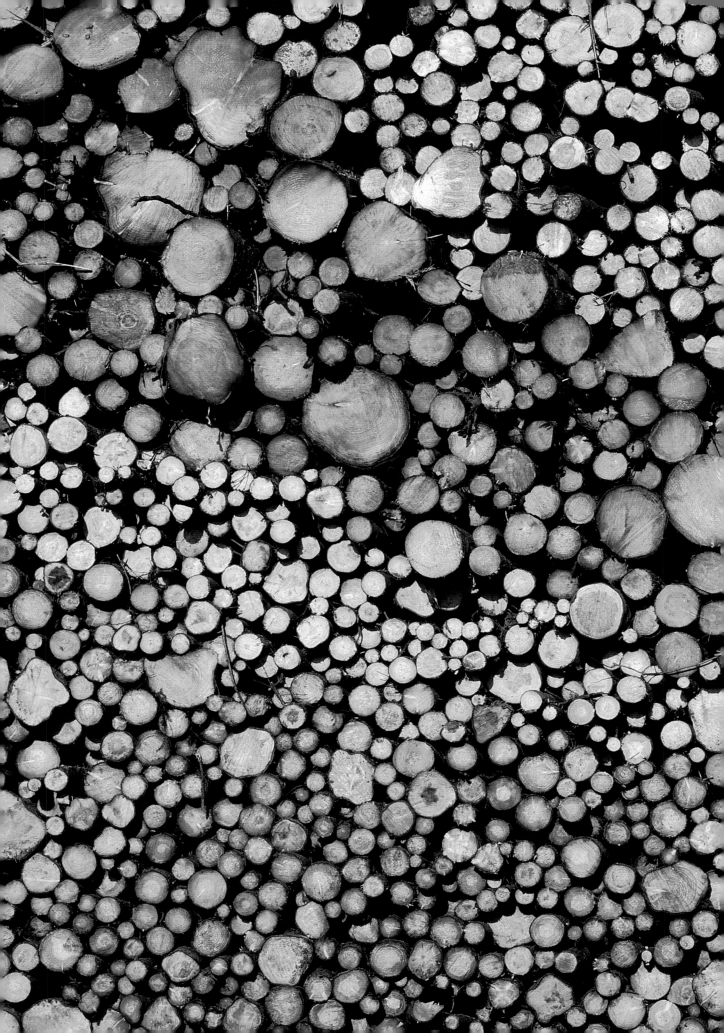

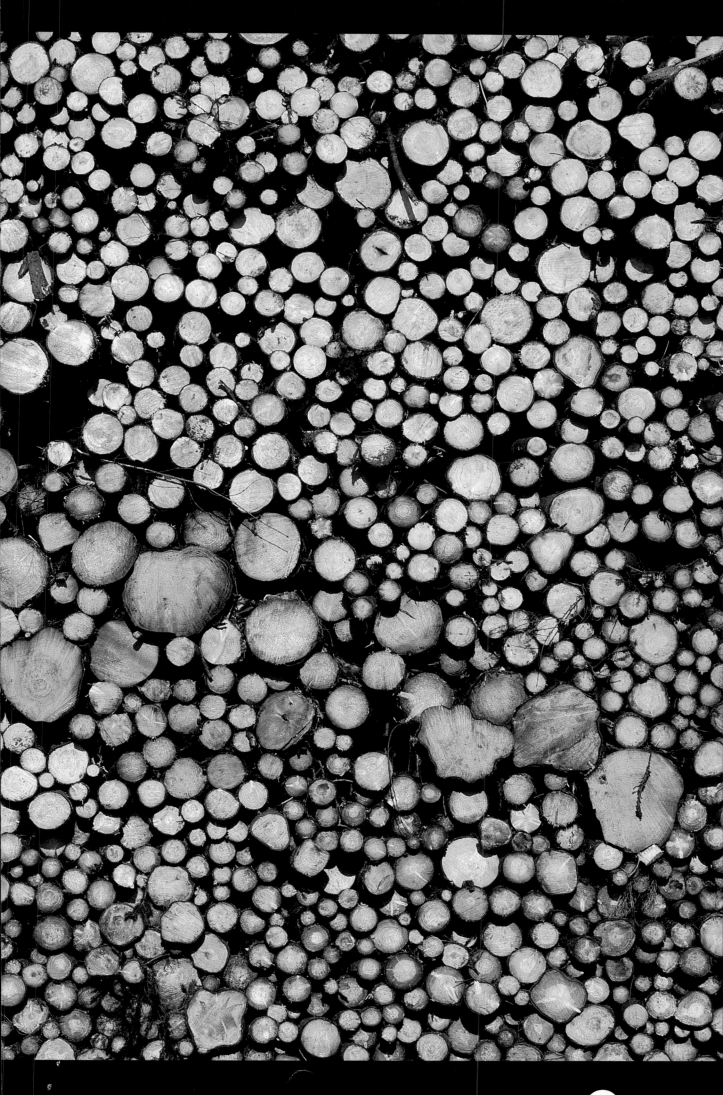

Even at the bottom of the sea, slow and steady wins the race!

  It's neither the hair, nor the beard...

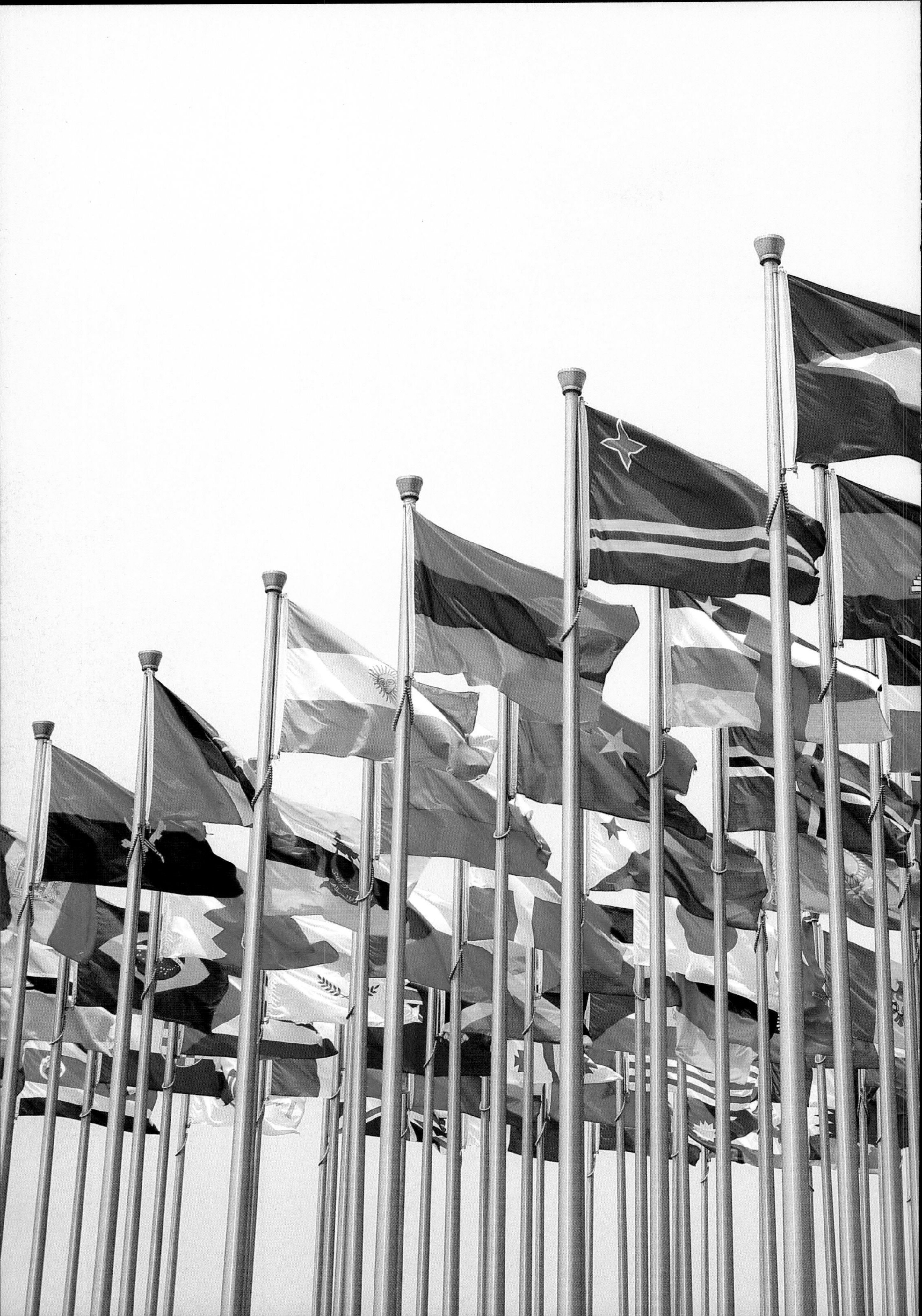

 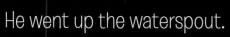

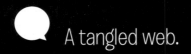

Turn over a new leaf.

Mighty strength in a tiny body.

Like searching for a needle in a haystack!

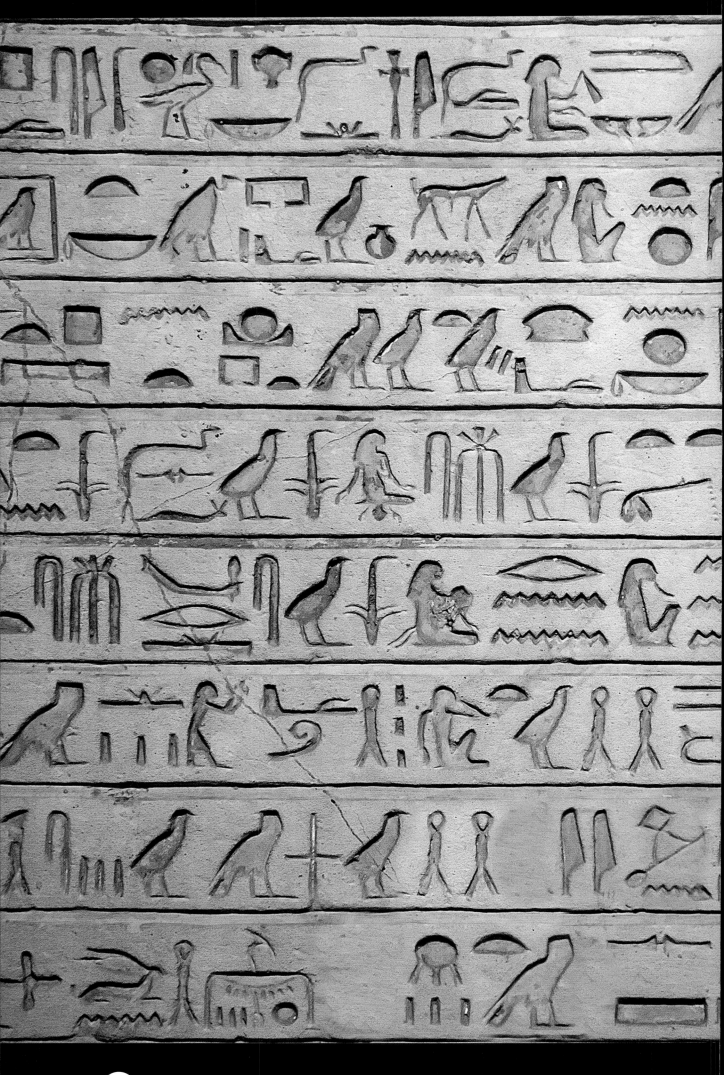

Tutankhamen in the Wild West.

It doesn't add up!

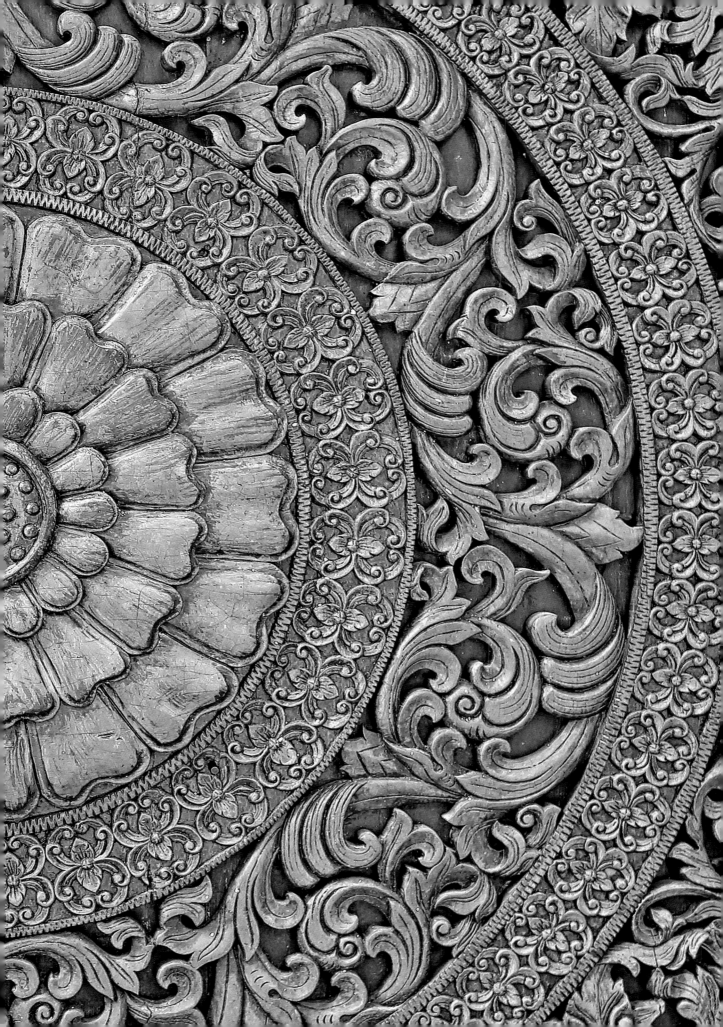

Saint Clicker, pray for us!

Cover

P. 4/5

P. 6/7

P. 8/9

P. 10/11

P. 12/13

P. 14/15

P. 16/17

P. 18/19

P. 20/21

P. 22/23

P. 24/25

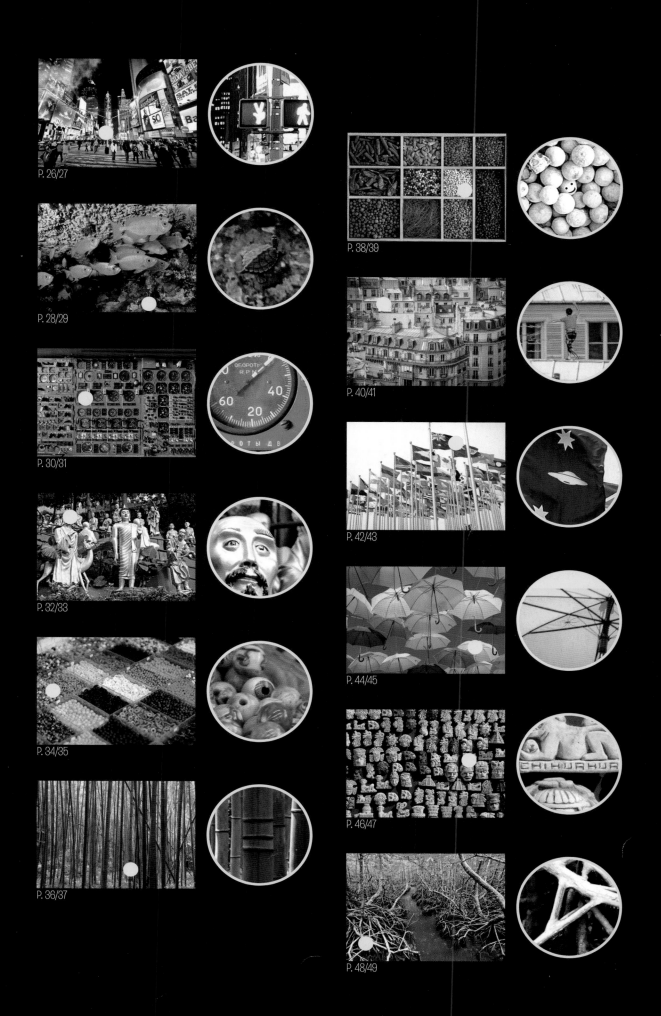

P. 26/27

P. 28/29

P. 30/31

P. 32/33

P. 34/35

P. 36/37

P. 38/39

P. 40/41

P. 42/43

P. 44/45

P. 46/47

P. 48/49

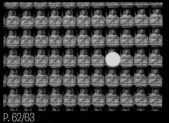

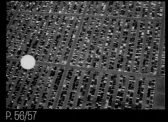

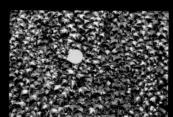
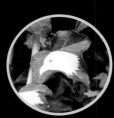

P. 74/75

P. 76/77

P. 78/79

P. 80/81

P. 82/83

P. 84/85

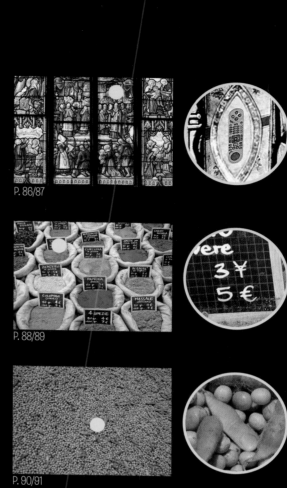

P. 86/87

P. 88/89

P. 90/91

PHOTO CREDITS

Cover: Mexican Masks ©sisqopote/Shutterstock.com

Interior: p.4 ©Cobalt88/coll. istockphoto/thinkstock.com; p.6 ©Thinkstock.com; p.8 Aerial View of Lima (Peru) ©Pablo Hidalgo/Shutterstock.com; p.10 ©Hal_P/Shutterstock.com; p.12 © TrotzOlga/coll. istockphoto/thinkstock.com; p.14 Stained glass window of St-Gervais-St Protais church, Paris, The Judgement of Solomon ©Zvonimir Atletic/Shutterstock.com; p.16 Island of Burano ©Korzhonov Danii/Shutterstock.com; p.18 Traffic jam in Beijing (China) ©TonyV3112/Shutterstock.com; p.20 ©Carsten Medom Madsen/Shutterstock.com; p.22 Manavagat Mosque, Antalya (Turkey) ©Sophie McAulay/Shutterstock.com; p.24 Containers in the port of Hong Kong ©Sergey Novikov/Shutterstock.com; p.26 Times Square, New York ©Andrey Bayda/Shutterstock.com; p.28 Common Bigeye Fish ©Rich Carey/Shutterstock.com; p.30 ©ID1974/Shutterstock.com; p.32 © sakio3p/coll. istockophoto/thinkstock.com; p.34 ©Chubykin Arkady/Shutterstock.com; p.36 © lo_409/Shutterstock.com; p.38 ©Elena Schweitzer/Shutterstock.com; p.40 Roofs of Paris seen from Notre-Dame © Robert Crumr/Shutterstock.com; p.42 ©ArtisticPhoto/Shutterstock.com; p.44 ©Hugo Felix/Shutterstock.com; p.46 Mayan wood handcrafts (Mexico) ©holbox/Shutterstock.com; p.48 Asian mangrove © saiko3p/Shutterstock.com; p.50 Manhattan, New York ©Songquan Deng/Shutterstock.com; p.52 ©Aleksandr Kurganov/Shutterstock.com; p.54 Collage of doors in Kiev (Ukraine) ©natalia_maroz/Shutterstock.com; p.56 ©Sodapix sodapix/Thinkstock.com; p.58 ©Viktor Gladkov/Shutterstock.com; p.60 ©Tatiana Grozetskaya/Shutterstock.com; p.62 ©Prasit Rodan/coll. istockphoto/thinkstock.com; p.64 Nasir ol Molk Mosque, Shiraz (Iran) ©JPRichard/Shutterstock.com; p.66 ©Flegere/Shutterstock.com; p.68 ©smuay/Shutterstock.com; p.70 ©swisshippo/coll. istockphoto/thinkstock.com; p.72 ©moodboard/thinkstock.com; p.74 Old Town, Prague (Czech Republic) ©Matthew Dixon/Shutterstock.com; p.76 ©thinkstock.com; p.78 ©donatas1205/Shutterstock.com; p.80 Statue of Liberty and Manhattan ©Joshua Haviv/Shutterstock.com; p.82 ©I love Photo/Shutterstock.com; p.84 ©blinow61/coll. istockphoto/thinkstock.com; p.86 Basilica of Our Lady of Bramble, Josselin (56) (France) ©Evgeny Shmulev/Shutterstock.com; p.88 ©Luciano Mortula/Shutterstock.com; p.90 ©rubenschaves/coll. istockphoto/thinkstock.com